≡ THE RAINY BREAD ≡

≡ POEMS FROM EXILE ≡

≡ BY ≡ MAJA TROCHIMCZYK ≡

≡ MOONRISE PRESS ≡ 2016 ≡

≡ COPYRIGHT NOTICE ≡

≡ TABLE OF CONTENTS ≡

≡ ≡ ≡ ≡ **PART IV ≡ THERE AND BACK** ≡ 35

≡ INTRODUCTION ≡

My previous book of war-themed poems, *Slicing the Bread* (Finishing Line Press, 2014) was prefaced with a rhetorical question: "If I were born in Warsaw, a city that lost 700,000 of its inhabitants, shouldn't I at least try to remember some of them? The 450,000 Jews and 250,000 non-Jewish Poles died before October 1944, when everyone left in Warsaw after the Uprising was expelled to deportee or labor camps, while the buildings of an empty city were dynamited into a sea of ruins." Then, the Soviets came...

This chapbook, written for the Kresy-Siberia Conference in Warsaw in September 2016, takes the story further east and around the world as it traces the displacement of deportees, their ordeals and miraculous survival stories. After the war, my parents, Aleksy Trochimczyk (25 September 1927 – 11 May 2001) and Henryka Teresa Trochimczyk, née Wajszczuk (16 December 1929 – 4 July 2013) came from provincial villages and towns in the Easter Borderlands, or Kresy, to study engineering at the Polytechnical University of Warsaw. They met while picking bricks off the ruined streets of Warsaw ("The Coat"). My father's family was Belarussian, with roots in the Ukraine and beyond; during the war, they were hungry and impoverished, but stayed on the family farm in Bielewicze, now in Poland.

My mother's family of Polish gentry and city folk living in Baranowicze and the surrounding area near Adam Mickiewicz's Nowogródek and the mythical lake of Świteź in what is now Belarus, was particularly affected by the deportations: the families Wajszczuk, Wasiuk, Ignatowicz, Gliński, Hordziejewski... Six poems are based on the memories of my family – grandmothers and aunts, mother and father. "Slicing the Bread" documents my Mom's obsession with saving and hoarding food, due to the years of war-time hunger.

"The Trap Door" commemorates my Dad's family survival in an isolated hamlet of Bielewicze near Gródek Białostocki. It was so close to the forest, it was constantly scoured for food by the "partisans" – but also fed the Germans, and the Soviets when they came. I admired the courage and resilience of my Belorussian Babcia Nina Trochimczyk, née Niegierysz.

"The Odds" is about my Mom's uncles, Catholic priests. Father Karol Wajszczuk (1887 – 1942) was a prisoner of the Lublin Castle since April 1940. He was moved to Sachsenhausen and then to Dachau, on December 14, 1940. He died on 28 May 1942 in the Castle Hartheim: in a gas chamber, originally built to exterminate the disabled in the Euthanasia program and later used to kill prisoners from Dachau. His father, Piotr, was the brother of Franciszek, the patriarch of the Wajszczuk-Trochimczyk family branch, and the father of Stanisław Marcin Wajszczuk (1895-1973), my grandfather from the village of Trzebieszów in Podlasie. Father Feliks Wajszczuk (b. 1902 – d. 1973), Karol's cousin, was in Sachenhausen, then in Dachau since 14 December 1940. He was liberated by Americans on 25 May 1945 and spent the rest of his life in a monastery in France.

In my poem, Karol and Feliks are paired up with another set of brothers, Artur Gold (1897-1943) and Henryk Gold (1902-1977), Jewish composers and musicians from Warsaw. Henryk survived by joining the musicians of the Second Corps of the Polish Army commanded by General Władysław Anders (1892-1970). The same group included Henryk Wars (Henry Vars, 1902-1977, "The Baton") and many other survivors.

My Grandma and her sisters, my Mom's maternal aunts, appear in several poems. Babcia Maria Anna Wajszczuk, born Wasiuk (1906-1973) in Baranowicze, wore her head high in the peasant village ("No Chicken") and taught me the skill of "Peeling the Potatoes."

Ciocia Tonia, or Antonina Glińska lost her husband to a Soviet bullet, and survived exile to Siberia, to return to Poland in 1954. Alas, her sons did not do as well: the older lost his life, drowning in Yenisey, the younger, indoctrinated in Soviet schools, lost his soul to a career in economics, the academe, and PZPR.

She is commemorated in "Ciocia Tonia" and her sister, Ciocia Irena, married name de Belina, appears in "Losing Irena." She was deported with her whole family, but came to America as an orphan, whose path from Siberia through Iran, Switzerland to Chicago and Albuquerque, New Mexico never ceased to amaze me.

Ciocia Jadzia, married name Hordziejewska, was resettled with her noble husband, Dominik in the early 1950s, and sent from their estate near Switez to a drab settlement house in Gdańsk-Oliwa, emptied of its German inhabitants (who, in turn, were resettled further West). Their portraits are in "Asters." More details may be found on the family tree, www.wajszczuk.v.pl, compiled by Waldemar Wajszczuk and Barbara Miszta, née Wajszczuk of Trzebieszów.

In addition to these rich and varied reprinted four poems based on my own childhood experiences in Warsaw, the capital of the socialist Polish People's Republic where I went to school and wondered about the shadow of the war: "Short Legs," "The Coat," "Standing Guard," and "What to Carry." Even though these poems focus on my native Warsaw, the intergenerational trauma that they express stems from my Mom's experience escaping from Soviet-occupied Baranowicze back to German-occupied Poland.

A sizeable portion of new poems commemorate deportees to Siberia and Central Asia. "Eyes on the Road" is based on an episode in the life of Roma King, author of *Footsteps in the Snow: A True Story of One Family's Journey Out of Siberia* (2010). Carlos (or Charlie) Stalgis ("Charlie, Who Did Not Cross") was born in Argentina and his family took the unsuccessful trek to the Polish border from the environs of Baranowicze ("Charlie, Who Did Not Cross"), while my grandparents, Mom, and uncle made it across the river Bug ("Starlight").

Baranowicze was also where the father of Lucyna Przasnyski had his roots ("Once Upon a Time in Baranowicze"). As a child deportee, Andrzej Dąbrowa took the infernal boat-ride along Amu Darya to the Aral Sea. Zofia Janczur had diamonds hidden in her shoes that saved the life of her whole family. Roma King waited for her Dad to come and get them, and he did ("Eyes on the Road").

I heard their stories during an event about *Sybiracy* organized for the Helena Modjeska Art and Culture Club in Los Angeles by Dorota Olszewska, herself a heir of Polish deportees to Siberia, repatriated to Szczecin (Stettin). On a sunny afternoon of June 5, 2016, they were joined by other survivors, Zofia Cybulska-Adamowicz, Wiesław Adamowicz and Elżbieta Nowicka in revealing their painful memories of Siberia or Kazakhstan ("On Trains and Tea," "A Piece of Good Advice…" and "Kasha.") The four pathways to California in "Five Countries in Venice" were shared by Carlos Stalgis, Roman Solecki, and Stefan Wisniowski, the founder of Kresy-Siberia Virtual Museum and the Facebook Group that brought us together.

Another poem, "Under African Sky" emerged from the biography of painter Julian Stanczak (b. 1928) who lost the use of his right hand in a Soviet gulag, and re-invented himself as an artist in the refugee camp in Masindi, Uganda. The "tiger's eye" I put in his hand is fictional but reflects the main idea of a re-oriented, yet immensely creative life. The Polish American Historical Association gave him theirs Creative Arts Prize in 2014 and thus I was introduced to his sublime and monumental and art.

At the Polish Film Festival in Los Angeles I watched an astounding documentary about Polish pilots training the new Pakistani Air Force. Established in 1947 during the division of India, the Moslem Pakistan needed help in creating its military; a task assisted by about 30 Polish pilots, veterans of the Battle of Britain. *Polish Eaglets Over Pakistan (Polskie orlęta na pakistańskim niebie)* presented their stories and the two vivacious female pilots particularly impressed me.

≡ Maja Trochimczyk

≡ ≡ ≡

I owe a huge debt of gratitude to all the individuals whose stories I transformed into poems. This book is meant to honor their sacrifice and document their resilience and survival. In addition to the members of my extended family, I'm especially grateful to Stefan Wiśniowski, and Sybiracy in California Zofia Cybulska-Adamowicz, Wiesław Adamowicz, Roma King, Zofia Janczur, doktor Bożena Gryglaszewska, Elżbieta Nowicka, Andrzej Dąbrowa, and Dorota Olszewski who encouraged them to share their painful recollections.

Sincere thanks is also due to the Finishing Line Press and its team of editors that published the original ten of these thirty poems in *Slicing the Bread* in 2014.

Finally, I would not be able to finish these poems without the assistance of fellow poets and writers whose comments have been as valuable to me, as is their friendship: Elżbieta Kańska, John Guzłowski, as well as the Westside Women Writers: Millicent Borges Accardi, Lois P. Jones, Georgia Jones-Davis, Susan Rogers, Kathi Stafford, Madeleine Butcher, and Sonya Sabanac. Thank you.

≡ Maja Trochimczyk

☰ PART I ☰
☰ DESTINATIONS ☰

≡ 1 ≡ WHAT TO CARRY ≡

You never know when the war will come,
her mother said. *You have to be ready.*
Most things are unimportant.
You must take your gold, your family jewels.
Diamonds will buy you food.
Gold will save your life. Forget silver, too heavy.
Take sturdy boots with two pairs of socks,
a warm, goose-down comforter on your back,
one picture, no books. Leave it all.
You will have to walk, sleep in a ditch, walk.
Pack lightly. What you carry, will protect you.
From starving, from freezing. That's what matters.
Goose-down and gold. Hunger and snow.

She still has her goose-down coverlet,
useless in California. Her mother squished it
into a suitcase the first time she came to visit.
The down came from geese plucked decades ago
in Bielewicze, by her Grandma, Nina.
Diamonds? She sold her rings
to pay for the divorce, keep the house
with pomegranates and orange trees.
Her shoes are useless too —
a rainbow of high heels in the closet.

☰ 2 ☰ STARLIGHT ☰

The Soviets came in 1939.
They shot her uncle in the street,
and took his widow, Aunt Tonia,
with their two sons to Siberia. All in 24 hours.

Her father did not wait. He sold what he could.
They went through the "green border"
back to his family near Lublin.
Germans were not half as bad.

Two pairs — a parent, a child — walking quietly
in a single file through deep snow drifts.
Long shadows on the sparkling, midnight white.
The guide took them in a boat across the river Bug.
Smooth, black water between brilliant banks.
Twisted tree branches, turning.

The moon hid behind clouds.
Stars scattered. On the other shore,
the guide told her to take off her coat.
He ripped out the lining, counted
the gold coins her mother had sown
into the seams. He tore apart her teddy bear,
took the jewels from his belly.

I got frostbite on my cheeks and hands that night.
Look at the spots, she told her daughter.
We had paid him already. You cannot trust
anyone, not anyone at all.

$\equiv$ 3 $\equiv$ CHARLIE, WHO DID NOT CROSS $\equiv$

We sit in a Venice restaurant
drinking Malbec and Napa Cabernet,
nibbling on roasted almonds and fried dates.

Charlie, or Carlos, is a stranger from Argentina
until he says: "My grandparents were caught
by Soviets while walking toward the river Bug,
to cross back to Poland."

— in 1940, the coldest winter in memory —
— endless plains of white snow along black water —
— walking single-file to leave one trail —
— covered with linen sheets to merge with the frozen
    landscape, under icy moonlight —

They did not make it. Soviets waited at the shore.
Six months in prison. A month on the train east,
to Siberia. The same old: hunger, gulag, cold.

Then, amnesty came, and freedom.
The Anders's Army took them through Iran,
Palestine, and the battlefields of Europe.
When it was over, a trans-Atlantic travel south.

Born in Argentina, he carried the past
of his family to California, where I listen,
bewildered by this twist of fate.

The same river, the same midnight fields
of snow, the same, coldest winter, the same
single-file footsteps. The same. All the same.

Only the ending's different. My mom,
an eight-year-old with her parents, brother,
made it to the boat hidden on the shore.

All the money stolen, they kept their lives
and frostbite as a memento of this crossing
in drifts of snow, on the way to safety in Podlasie.

His grandparents did not make it. Or maybe,
they did. Caught, imprisoned, they reached
the land of tangoes. Their Argentina
of freedom and wild dreams.

≡ 4 ≡ FIVE COUNTRIES IN VENICE ≡

Four people, five countries connected
through the dark cord of the sixth — once
 and always an evil empire, one among the many.
(They all are evil now, in this new world
order of endless wars.)

Poland — the anchor of a shared language
that has not perished yet, with rye bread,
sweet butter and buckwheat honey,
Chopin, Matejko and Mickiewicz,
wildflowers, nostalgia, and rain.
The Alma Mater of grief.

Excluded from the Victory Parade in 1945
by the United Kingdom, so United —
it took up the Polish soldiers' offer to defend it;
so United — it expelled them to the ends
of its crumbling empire after the battles were done —

To Canada — the vast terrains with open borders,
clean air and water, safe streets, and welcome.
The best country in the world, if you are willing to brave
the constant cold, your breath freezing in your nose –

To Australia — of red earth and animals that prove
the creator's sense of humor, surely made in jest.
A dream-scape for dark-skinned, silent sages.
A penal colony for London thugs and whores.
A shelter for those with nowhere else to go
when the global cataclysm was over —

To Argentina — where they dance the tango
and mourn the twenty thousands of the "desaparecidos"
while giving refuge to executioners and their prey.
They would not know, no, really, would not –
the two hundred thousand that disappeared
without a trace from the plains of Wołyń.

They would not think of one, two millions —
who is counting? — Polish civilians, deported, gone.
The Queen expelled the former soldiers,
once allies, then a ballast of unwanted guilt
to California — almost an island, an archipelago
of its own. Each mind — a cosmos of invention.
Each heart — a universe of masks.

Here, we meet on the bright shores of the Pacific
in the Republic of the other Venice. We sip
the Russian Valley Cabernet and ponder
the messy handiwork of power-drunk Furies
and the impassioned, patient Fates. This tapestry
is almost done. *Lachesis, Clotho* tangled up the skein.
All we can do is wait for their sister, *Atropos*
to show her mercy by cutting our threads.

In greek mythology Atropos was one of the three Moirai, goddesses of fate & destiny. Her Roman equivalent was Morta. atropos was the oldest of the Three Fates & was known as "inflexible" or "inevitable". It was Atropos who chose the mechanism of death and ended the life of mortals by cutting their thread and Lachesis who measured the length, Cleo who spun the thread.

≡ 5 ≡ EYES ON THE ROAD ≡

"Daddy" — she says — "Daddy will find us.
I am sure, he will come back."

The road there and back was the hardest.
First, the separation. Then, not knowing
where this trek through tall, foreboding forests
and misty plains was taking them.
Distances beyond imagination. Nothing like
the long-lost Poland, where each turn
of the road opened a new vista, as lovable as home.

This alien, hostile expanse of sharp grass and thickets,
blurred by clouds of mosquitoes and black flies
that cut triangles in the skin to get to your flesh.
Eat you alive — just like piranhas. You knew better
than to venture beyond the walls of your rotten hut.

There were no wires, fences were not needed.
How could they leave? And… where
would they go? It was impossible to find a way
out of this freezing, humid Hades.

"Daddy" — she says — "I knew
Daddy would come back and find us."

And he did, she writes in her book, page by page
of adventures of a lifetime, months of hunger
and cold beyond what anyone could expect.

"Daddy" — she says — "my Daddy has come back."

≡ 6 ≡ THE BATON ≡

He knows how to play his instruments.
Playing saved his life, not once, not twice. Forever.

The harmonica amused soldiers at the checkpoint
so he was waved on – идите музыкант, уже пошли.
The violin bought him food and lodging, the peasants
gathered for an impromptu dance to his tunes.

He found his way to a uniform with Polish eagles.
Its rough, scratchy wool more precious than tuxedos
with silk shirts and cravats of the bandleader
conducting foxtrots, tangoes in Warsaw's cabarets.

Musicians played for him then, and they play now.
He holds the baton. Again, the sounds float up,
move crowds to tears, dissipate in clear air.

The tune is different. This one marches along
with the soldiers' boots, treading red poppies,
across the battlefields, on to Warsaw, home.

≡ 7 ≡ **DIAMONDS** ≡

Elegant, in a one-of-a-kind silver necklace
and a green silk shawl — the uniform
of a sophisticated lady, a museum volunteer.
Today, she takes us on a tour of her past.

She had diamonds in her shoes —
hidden in the heels, to be exact.

They took one out to pay the driver
of a warm wagon, one — for a bag of rice,
a large bag, this diamond fed them for a month.
Diamond by diamond, they crossed Siberia.
Diamond by diamond, they found a way out.

An artist's soul, she is a docent at the Bowers.
She loves the piano. Of the exhibits,
the Tsarist Treasures were the best.
She has no diamonds now. The earrings,
Brooches, bracelets of her Mother's,
Grandma's, were her ticket into this life.

She still remembers the sparkling jewels
her Mom wore to a recital –
the white wool coat with pearly buttons,
a silver fox draped casually off her arm.

She so loved Chopin. She still loves Chopin.

Lost in the diamond cascades of the notes

arising off the keyboard to float upwards
to the diamond brilliance of the stars,
she thinks of diamonds, pure light crystals
that she walked on in her black shoes,
leaving Siberia, for the ever-brighter
jewels of California winter sky.

☰ PART II ☰
☰ THERE & NOWHERE ☰

≡ 8 ≡ THE ODDS ≡

Her mother's uncles, two of them
went to Sachsenhausen. One came back, one did not.
It was a family game of sorts, others played it too.
Only one could survive: Karol or Feliks,
Artur or Henryk — one could win
if he had boots that fit, strength
to stand, walk, and carry a load of stones
from place to place, back and forth,
day in, day out.

They were betrayed on April 28, 1940.
The Home Army soldiers in their units
went to their deaths at Auschwitz.
They were priests. With the numbers
of the Beast tattooed on their forearms:
Karol — 25746 first, 22572 in Dachau, later.
Feliks — 22732 in Dachau, since December 14, 1940.

Caught far behind the new Soviet borders
Artur came home to Warsaw, when the bombs
stopped falling, Henryk travelled further
to test his good luck.

Would you guess who died on the 28th of May, 1942?
Who survived malaria experiments, advancing
Nazi science? Who was selected for
the "invalids' transport" to the gas chambers
at Hartheim Castle? Who was liberated,
strangely alive, when the Americans
finally came?

≡ 9 ≡ WOŁYŃ ≡

Some say 70 thousands.
Some say 150 thousands.
Some say 200 thousands.
Who knows.

1600 or 300 was enough
to imprint the name of a different village
onto the memory of the world.

Before IDs, passwords and credit cards,
Before the global surveillance machine
started to count every thought, every photo —
their births and weddings
were recorded in the church register
incinerated, after they and their houses
were burnt to ash.

Death in the flames —
Death by the bullet —
Death by the blade —
and the baton — and bare hands.

They lived and planted, carried wreaths
in procession in harvest festivals, danced
and laughed on cold October nights.

Gone now, forgotten, and uncounted.
Whole families, generations, gone.

Like leaves on white birch trees
that blaze in the last display of color
before rotting in the rain, disintegrating
into the ground.

Their land has other owners now
Their houses, barns and hamlets — erased.
Their village roads ploughed over.

We know some names.
We have some photos of some homes.
We even made a list of losses,
places. We may go back,
if we are lucky, look through
the rubble, dig out one brick.

Gone to the stars. Birch leaves of autumn.
Lost and forgotten, the Poles of Wołyń
will still shine bright.

≡ 10 ≡ KOŁYMA ≡

Who knows how many?

The pit was dark, still darker at the bottom,
deep as the gates of hell. Its demon's mouth wide
open to devour row after row of bright young men.

Who knows their faces now?
The corn-blue eyes sparkling with tears and laughter.
The closely cropped soldier's dark blond hair.

Down, down they went
to the bottomless pits of Kołyma
for Stalin's diamonds, uranium for his bombs.

> Down, down they went
> to the boundless hell of Kołyma
> for Stalin's riches, his bombs, and his revenge.

They lost the fight for Poland's sacred freedom
They knew how precious independence was, how rare.

They kept on fighting when enemies became allies.
Their lives sold on a global market of slaves.

> Down, down they went
> To the bottomless mines of Kołyma
> For Stalin's diamonds, uranium for his bombs.

☰ 11 ☰ AMU DARYA ☰ *Oxus in latin/Greek*
Vaksu = Sanskrit

Thank God, I've never seen the shores
Of Amu Darya, the deadly stretches
of hot sand lining both sides of the river
all the way to the horizon. Thank God.

The boat of deportees slowly makes its way
up to the inland Aral Sea. Very slowly.
Crowded on old wood planks and rusty iron
of the rickety deck, they are sardines
in a can with the top opened
to the merciless Amu Darya's sun.

All night, the boy lies next to a dying girl
wrapped in blankets, crying — crying — crying —
moaning through this starless shroud.

The old man's crying too, as he tells his story,
again a helpless boy who cannot silence her screams,
or ease her pain. For more than sixty years, he's heard
her voice, he's woken up in the middle of Amu Darya,
under the cruel, burning, foreign sun.

There, he is awake and gets up quickly
to show the guards that, still alive,
he can breathe and stand up straight,
despite the weight of that pitiless night,
spent huddled to the dying girl.

They pick her body up and throw her
off the boat onto the pristine whiteness
of the sand. She falls — and falls — and falls
into a lifeless heap among the dead,
discarded like the kitchen refuse, left to rot
under the surgical glare of Amu Darya's sun.

She has no face, no name, just this moaning.
No grave — her wrapped body lies unburied
with all the others who had died that night.
No time to let the people off the vessel.
No time to dig the graves. Their floating grave
has to continue on its aimless journey,
creeping along the empty shores.

No food, no water — just the heat
is left and the pervasive stench of death.

Thank God, I've never seen
the shores of Amu Darya —
its piles of bones on salty sand.

Only one tenth survived the way.

☰ 12 ☰ SHAMBHALA ☰

Do children who die on the way
get to carry bejeweled parasols in a Tibetan heaven?

Is Siberia too far from Shambhala
for the bedraggled orphans to enter through
its golden doorways, glistening with ten thousand
ornaments, more precious than the treasures
of a galaxy with ten billion suns?

Are they too dirty and sick to walk on a pathway
prepared for the birth of the Buddha —
scented with sandalwood water, adorned
with an unsurpassed multitude of precious gems.

When the Buddha was born, the Earth
moved six ways, the wise man said.

Did it move at least once to mark your passage?

When you rolled in pain and moaned
until the blessed moment of relief?
Gave your last breath like a crystal cloud
in frozen Siberian air? Slipped away
from a nightmarish dream? Convulsed
in a sudden burst of gunfire, a bullet straight
through your heart? Froze to death in a convoy?
Fainted on the floor of the dirty railroad car?

There was no hooting of owls, they say,
when the great Shakyamuni Buddha
was born. Sweet sounding music floated
through in a myriad of flowering orchards,
with the rarest fruit on gemstone trees.

Did you hear an owl hoot when you died?
Oh, hungry child of gulags, the child of Siberia —
Did the Earth move? Were there parasols, or owls?

That's what I want to know, when we meet again.

≡ 13 ≡ **REFLECTION** ≡

You cannot save the life of someone
who does not want to live.

Remember this, young boy of Amu Darya.
Remember this, brave girl of Siberian trains.

Remember —

And let go of the pain-filled moaning,
Let go of the rasping breath of the dying girl,

Let go of the dull, glazed eyes of your brother,
Sweating his last on the prison cot.

Let go — let go — let go —
my dear — you must let go —
You cannot save a life,
except your own.

The opaque energy, memories, this cloud
has strength enough to kill you.

So lock away these pearls of unshed tears,
forget the precious jewels of distress.

Remember this, remind yourself each morning:
you cannot save a life, except your own.

≡ 14 ≡ A PIECE OF GOOD ADVICE TO ≡ ≡ STUFF IN THE HOLE IN THE WALL≡

"Be quiet, walls have ears" —
in this village of barracks and sand.

The walls of rough tree-trunks,
with gaps filled with moss, or mud, or anything
that would keep the cruel blizzard out.

It was dárk, dark and cold — that's all I remember.

Dark, cold and endless — the hours all the same,
slipping one into another.

Days go by quietly, full of dreams
of fresh strawberries, apple cider, piles
of blintzes dripping with molten butter by the stove.

One wrong word and you are taken –
somewhere that's even darker, worse

"Be quiet, then, these walls have ears.
You have one life. Be quiet. *Non?*"

≡ 15≡ A PILOT IN PAKISTAN ≡

She learned to fly to have wings —
to look down at the rolling waves of mountains,
the geometry of fields outlined by rivers,
dotted by lakes, to see where clouds
were born, and where they were going.

Now she teaches soldiers of a foreign army
how to fly and kill, kill and fly away, unharmed.

They call it the dogfight, as in, dog eats dog, the bigger dog,
the faster dog, the dog with sharper teeth. The dogs of war.

Six years was enough.
Enough of this war.

She lost her home, her house, her childhood.
She has no future. Alone, wearing blond curls
and the tight, belted uniform of a pilot
she's teaching soldiers in a Muslim country
how to fly to war.

☰ 16 ☰ UNDER AFRICAN SKY ☰

— *amber and coral* —

— *ruby and carnelian* —

He looks at the brightness of the African sky,
The blazing sunset above the plains of Uganda
His eyes follow the pattern of light and shadow
on the savanna's tall grass; dark lines cutting
into light on the flank of the zebra —
so like a humble donkey he remembers
from home, except for the extravagant, geometric
boldness of the stripes, shining bright.

Blinding his eyes, used to Siberian darkness
in dim interiors of cold, musty prison huts —
he admires the play of gold stripes inside
the tiger's eye — a stone his teacher gave him
for protection and good luck. How it shifts
with each turn, different, yet the same —
lines upon lines of light, liquid light.

The richness stays under his eyelids
as he twists and turns the tiger's eye
in his one good hand, left — while the other,
a useless appendage, hangs limply at his side
since the beating in the Soviet prison camp
shattered his dream of music, silenced
the honey-rich tones of his cello.

He found a different-flavored honey
in the richness of African sunsets,
the stripes of tiger's eye that awoke
his talent for capturing the undulating lines
and blazing hues on majestic canvas,
moving in the rhythm of wild planes
out of Africa, into fame.

  — *amber and topaz* —

  — *gold, bronze, and light,* —

  — *so much light.* —

☰ PART III ☰
☰ THE HUNGER DAYS ☰

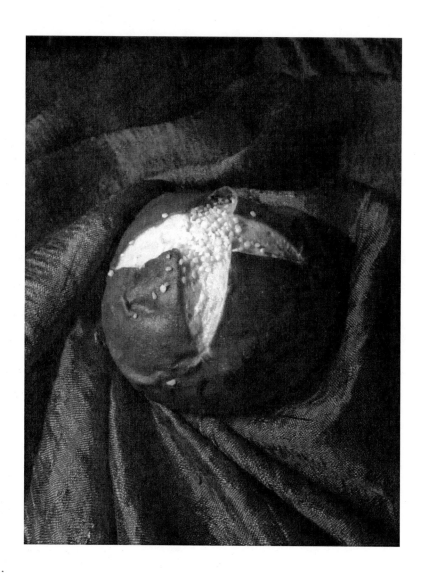

≡ 17 ≡ KASHA ≡

What's for breakfast? — *Kasha.*
For lunch? — *Kasha.* For dinner? — *Kasha.*

— You are so lucky and you don't know it.

We used to eat the soup of potato peels
with dark bread, its flour mixed with sawdust and sand.

On a good day in the summer we could pick
a handful of fresh greens. Dandelions and nettle
were the best — well chopped, refreshing.

We did not go out much in the spring
when the black cloud of mosquitoes
and flies could kill a bear.

A breakfast, lunch and dinner of a warm,
well-cooked *Kasha,* is a meal straight
from the other side of heaven,
such as I never knew
until peace came.

☰ 18 ☰ THE TRAP DOOR ☰

His father died of pneumonia in 1939.
The boy, the man of the house, could not go to school
after that. Only in winter, walking across six kilometers
of snow-covered fields on a hungry stomach.
Too little food on the farm.

The partisans, Germans — everyone came to steal it.
What the Germans left, the partisans ate.
They all had guns. Gleaming Walthers.
Battered Kalashnikovs.

At the end, Soviets came. No boots, no coats.
Rubber soles cut out from tires, tied
to their legs with bits of string. They begged
for potato peels to eat, old newspapers to stuff
into their tattered uniforms, keep warm.

They never found a second food pantry
under the bed of his ancient great-uncle.
Nobody looked for the trap door
beneath the grey mountain of pillows,
suffused with the old man's sweat.

The third piglet was hidden in a grass-covered
bunker, dug out in secret behind the barn.
They fed it by moonlight until the spring.
They ate everything, one glass jar per week:
head, tail, skin, bones for the soup.

Long after the war, his mother showed him
the gleaming hinges, rough wooden planks
a square cut in the floor, covered with
a homespun rug. That's how they survived.

≡ 19 ≡ SLICING THE BREAD ≡

Her mother's hunger. One huge pot of hot water
with some chopped weeds — *komesa, lebioda* —
she taught her to recognize their leaves,
just in case — plus a spoonful of flour
for flavor. Lunch for twenty people
crammed into a two-bedroom house.

The spring was the worst–flowers, birdsong,
and nothing to eat. You had to wait
for the rye and potatoes to grow. The pantry
was empty. She was hungry. Always hungry.
She ate raw wheat sometimes. Too green,
The kernels she chewed — still milky — made her sick.

Thirty years after the war,
her mother stashed paper bags with sliced, dried bread
on top shelves in her Warsaw kitchen.
Twenty, thirty bags — enough food for a month.
Don't ever throw any bread away, her mother said.
Remember, war is hunger.

Every week, her mother ate *dziad* soup —
fit for a beggar, made with crumbled wheat buns,
stale sourdough loaves, pieces of dark rye
soaked in hot tea with honey.
She liked it. She wanted to remember
its taste.

≡ 20 ≡ PEELING THE POTATOES ≡

Her Grandma showed her how to hold
the knife, cut a straight, narrow strip,
keeping the creamy flesh nearly intact,
ready for the pot of boiling water.

Don't throw away any food. The old refrain.
My sisters, Tonia and Irena lived on potato peels
in Siberia. She is confused. She knows
Ciocia Tonia — glasses on the tip of her nose,
perfectly even dentures — but Irena? Who is that?

They were all deported to Siberia. Not sure how
Irena's parents died — of typhus, or starvation, maybe?
They used to pick through garbage heaps,
look for rotten cabbage, kitchen refuse
to cook and eat. They cooked and ate anything
they found under the snow, frozen solid.

The water's boiling. *Babcia* guides her hand:
You have to tilt the cutting board
toward the pot, slide the potatoes in.
Don't let them drop and splash you.

What happened next? *The orphaned children*
went with the Anders's Army and the Red Cross
to Iran, Switzerland, Chicago. The kitchen
fills with memories. Mist above the stove.

Grandma piles up buttery, steaming,
mashed potatoes on her plate. *Eat, child, eat.*

Ten years later, Aunt Irena came to visit.
She looked like Grandma, only smaller.
Her legs were crooked.

≡ PART IV ≡
≡ THERE AND BACK ≡

≡ 21 ≡ OF TRAINS AND TEA ≡

I remember trains and horse-drawn wagons –
being all cooped up in a pile of blankets.
Was it so far? Were we going in circles?

Давайте, пойдем — Хорошо, хорошо

Yes, I remember the hypnotic noise
of train wheels on the tracks.
Piercing, repetitive, permeating your body
and echoing in your brain. To the border,
two days waiting, then a different patter
of the Russian, broader tracks.

It was dark and cold and I was afraid.

Yes, I was, too. I did not know where
we were going, what dark hut was destined
to be our home for who knows how many years.

The road there was so long.
Stopping and starting.
As if it would never end.

The sad train whistle, the calls
of the guards, that's what's real now –
as they sit, sipping tea out of fine bone china
on the patio scented with orange blossoms
of the glorious California spring.

Хорошо, хорошо —
мы готовы – давайте —
хорошо

≡ 22 ≡ ONCE UPON A TIME ≡
≡ IN BARANOWICZE ≡

This city is a cipher without a face. Just splinters
of images caught on paper. The blustery winter
street with a round poster stand just like in Warsaw.
The opulent interior of the photographer's studio
with a bearskin for naked babies, a mahogany stand
for First-Communion girls, with rosaries and lace gloves.
Flowers for Marshall Piłsudski, tightly held in a fist
by the prettiest girl with locks of curly hair.

That's all. No childhood street corners, no velvet
and muslin curtains of the family home.
No church bells. Some forgotten shrines.

This was the site of battles. In 1916 — 100,000 dead,
far less than the 700,000 of Verdun. Known to no-one.
Still, each life matters. Once more: Baranowicze
where, in forty-two, forty-eight priests and teachers
were murdered in cold blood. By Germans? Soviets?

The German rule meant disappearing in the ghetto.
Half of the town gone. The Soviet rule equaled
crowded freight trains to Kazakhstan, Irkutsk, and
Arkhangelsk. For me, this city is a cipher,
only existing as the birthplace of my Mom.

Lucyna tells a different story — bus trips to Świteź,
Mickiewicz's poems, silver ponds at Grandpa's farm.

Spring: white bells of the lilies of the valley,
picked by the bucket.. Summer: gold fields,
sunflower heads as huge as dinner plates.
Autumn: the Soviets came. Nothing
could save them from deportation, ruin —
you know — the usual.

≡ 23 ≡ CIOCIA TONIA ≡

Only a pear tree
between fields of sugar beets and corn.
Sweet pears — that's all left from the house,
barn and orchard. The farm where she raised
her sons, milked her cows, and baked her bread.

Only a pear tree. A lone memento
standing forlorn in an August field.

They ploughed it over — the village church and bus stops,
the neighbors' corrals, where their horses used to neigh.
They ploughed it over — her garden of herbs and cosmos,
its fragile lace of leaves and petals kissed by sunlight,
a flower-dream — she used to think, and loved it,
the effervescent beauty of the past.

It is not painful now, just surprising,
her whole life gone, and one tree left.
No name of her ancestral village on the maps.

The worst was when she saw her neighbors
running with news, her husband shot
in the middle of the dusty village road.

No time for grief, she saved her tears for later.
The orders came at once, a day to pack
for a long train ride to an unfamiliar city
near a river she never longed to see.

They said, pack wisely — the warmest clothes,
boots, pillows. As much food as you can carry.
Where you are going, there is nothing,
except for freezing breath and bitter cold.

Only a pear tree
in an empty field of stubble.

Only a pearl tree
in her golden field of dreams.

≡ 24 ≡ ASTERS ≡

Her mother's aunt, *Ciocia Jadzia* works in a kiosk in Oliwa
selling papers and razor blades in a ruined city
of charcoal buildings and five-year plans
She hides the best blades for her faithful clients
in the kiosk on the way to the Cathedral

where angels with puffy wooden cheeks
triumphantly blow their golden trumpets
walls and benches shake with the majesty of Bach
the gold-starred ceiling shimmers
in summer evening cold

The music of the seaside vacation heals the grey hours
of the girl, sitting in the kiosk, selling matches and tickets
after Ciocia Jadzia goes home to cook dinner
for her silent husband, drunk artist son

She works — Uncle Dominik, a proud nobleman
in a top hat and a black Sunday coat
walks through Oliwa's parks
with his last, prize-winning Holstein cow
He grieves the loss of his estates — the life he had had
before that fateful train ride from the East

He still sees the red-roofed manor with a white porch
bronze oak leaves scattered on the gravel path
silver gray of Lake Świteź
golden rye fields before the harvest

He walks home to rusty bricks pocked by bullet holes,
smoke-dark hallways, and a burst of color
in the courtyard where asters tremble —
in last evening breeze –

a bouquet of fallen stars

≡ 25 ≡ NO CHICKEN ≡

Ko-ko-ko — the clucking of hens
is a homey refrain of my California morning.
Some neighbors got themselves a chicken coop
in our sunlit village on the outskirts
of a grand metropolis.

Ko-ko-ko — the sounds take me back
to vacations with Grandma. Too proud
to stoop down to the level of peasants, she
wore a thick apron and gloves for work outside,
took it all off every time she walked into the house.

She could kill a rooster swiftly with one strike of the axe
and peel off the feathers in a gruesome spectacle
of steaming blood and guts.

Ko-ko-ko — dark orangey goo of the egg yolks
colored with a gold hue the best Easter *babka,*
the muslin one, so tall and delicate that children
were sent out while it cooled atop feathered pillows
in the locked bedroom.

We ate the rooster soup, *rosół,* with home-made noodles
Sliced with the sharpest knife, from a sheet of dough
dried in the same room on clean white linen towels.

Ko-ko-ko — the hen measures time as I think of *Babcia.*
In her city youth, she never touched a chicken,

a fashionable niece of a rich landowner,
she wore her pearls and an ostrich-feather hat
for the Sunday ide to church, while the farmhands
worked as hard as she does now.

A lone lady in a peasant village, she learned
how to pick the eggs and bake a *babka*.
She has her crystal vases full of lilac, still,
but she knows how to cut off the rooster's head
with one blow, how to cook her unexcelled *rosół*
with fresh carrots she picks from the garden,
like a lady, in gloves.

≡ 26 ≡ SHORT LEGS ≡

Niech żyje nam Towarzysz Stalin
On usta słodsze ma od malin —

Her mother, still a girl, murmurs the refrain
waiting for the soles of her worn boots to be fixed.
Her only pair, she marched them right off.
The old shoemaker smiles gently.

Don't sing that, child. These are all lies.
Stalin is worse than Hitler. He killed thirty million.
Hitler — ten.

She remembers his words
when she stands at attention with her class
for the mandatory five minutes of crying
after *Batiuszka* Stalin, the beloved Father
of Nations, died.

The truth will come out, the old man had assured her.
Lies have short legs, don't go far.

Sixty years later, she reads about Captain Pilecki,
the Auschwitz volunteer who escaped

to warn the Allies. He fought on:
for truth, for freedom.

Condemned by Stalinist courts, executed.
It took sixty years for a pardon
and the Order of the White Eagle.

A voice in the desert.
Nobody wanted to believe.

NOTE: Incipit from the songbook of ZMP, Union of Polish Youth:
Long live, Our Dear Comrade Stalin / Your lips are sweeter than raspberries.

≡ 27 ≡ THE COAT ≡

The young woman in a faded black-and-white photo
laughs with her head tilted, buttons undone
on her military coat. *You look fashionable, Mom,*
when was it taken? The girl looks up, her mother frowns.

They took a break from passing bricks, cleaning up
Warsaw streets — tunnels among mountains of rubble.
Brick-by-brick, hand-to-hand, long chains of students.
Sundays, evenings. They found bodies sometimes.
Mom sighs.

I met your Dad rebuilding Warsaw with our bare hands.
But the coat? I hated this beet-shade monster.
Hideous. Rough. A soldier's coat from UNRA.
I helped Babcia take it apart, wash the pieces,
dye them — from army green to beet-root.

Fifteen years. When the fabric wore out,
she undid the seams, turned it inside out,
sewed the pieces back together just like
her own Mom showed her. Stitch by stitch.

Her stockings were hand-sewn, too,
from soldiers' *onuce* — long bandages
for wrapping feet in heavy boots.

Take two, make two seams — Voila! You look like
Marilyn Monroe in "Some Like it Hot!"

Mom sighs again. *Don't ask,*
I'll never teach you how to sew.

≡ 28 ≡ STANDING GUARD ≡

At a tombstone for strangers
she shivers in the freezing rain of April.
A white shirt, pleated navy skirt, school sweater.
The longest hour. Red tie. An ugly beret.

Not allowed to move, sit, turn, frown,
or scratch her nose. Not allowed
to talk to the other girl. No smiling.
Eyes fixed, looking straight ahead.

The longest hour. This is how the dead
consume the living. Reverse cannibalism.
Would she have volunteered,
had her parents told her?

Two great uncles, priests at Dachau:
one relieved of his ills in a gas chamber,
one liberated, with his body, spirit broken.
A Home Army fighter killed in Auschwitz.

Two others hanged in the Lublin Castle.
One survivor of Majdanek and Gross Rosen.
Three siblings from the Warsaw Uprising,
buried under ruins in September 1944.

Those who perished in the Soviet gulag.
That officer shot in the Katyń forest.
The list goes on and on. Is that what
a ten-year-old is meant to learn?

≡ 29 ≡ LOSING IRENA ≡

I think we lost Irena, we lost her for good.
She retired, moved to Albuquerque,
taught schoolchildren about the camps
of Siberia and disappeared.

Tonia was looking for her, writing letters.
Basia wrote too, to all of Irena's children in Colorado,
Chicago and Utah. Nobody answered. Maybe they moved.

Irena's gone. She barely walked, shuffling her crooked
frostbitten legs, worse for the wear after decades
in Chicago, the Windy City. Those legs never forgot
Siberia and the train ride to Kazakhstan.

First, she was taken, with her mother, brother,
put on the train east. They went so far they must
have encircled the Earth three times over.
Siberia was a different world.

Then, she disappeared into herself, calm and quiet.
She stopped talking at the deathbed of her Mom.
It was not fair, she thought, that Mom was dying,
nothing ever would be.

She could not speak until she saw the ocean,
bright sparks of sunrays sliding off the waves.

And now she's gone, her memory's dissolving
in amber reflections of the setting sun.

≡ 30 ≡ **LANGUAGE** ≡

—— is all there is, all you take with you when you go
from country to country, carried by the winds of change.
The merciless gale of history blows you backward
to the time before homes were homes,
before safety, before love.

Hold on. Language is all there is. You'll leave
your sentimental treasures — a miniature
flower vase from your cloistered Godmother,
brown like her Franciscan habit and warm eyes.

A worn sapphire set in the ornate gold ring
Dad bought in Moscow for your Mom's engagement —
scarred by work and trouble, washing dishes,
work, always more work.

A suitcase of photos you are too raw
with grief to open — one day, you say,
I promise, I'll do it, one day.

Language is all there is. Words slip back
under the avalanche of hours. What you took
was yours then, what is theirs now?

Rough tones of Polish mountain village resound
through the gilded salons of an L.A. mansion.

They speak a 17th century peasant dialect in Quebec.

Out of one accent, not yet in another,
you sound foreign everywhere, to everyone.

You keep your word in-between kingdoms.

One day, you'll find the treasures.

Language is all there is
until your New Day comes.

≡ THE END ≡

≡ ABOUT THE AUTHOR ≡

Photo by Susan Rogers, 2016

MAJA TROCHIMCZYK, Ph.D., is a poet, music historian, photographer, and non-profit director, born in Poland and living in California. She published six books on music and five volumes of poems: *Rose Always - A Court Love Story, Miriam's Iris,* and *Slicing the Bread: Children's Survival Manual in 25 Poems,* plus two anthologies, *Chopin with Cherries* and *Meditations on Divine Names* that offer "rich poetic material selected and collected with great sensitivity" (Grażyna Kozaczka, *Polish Review,* 58/4, 2014). Hundreds of her articles and poems appeared in English, Polish, as well as in German, French, Spanish Serbian, and Chinese translations, in such journals as *Angel City Review, The Loch Raven Review, Epiphany Magazine, Lily Review, Ekphrasis Journal, Quill and Parchment, Magnapoets, SGVGPQ, The Cosmopolitan Review, The Scream Online, The Original Van Gogh's Ear Anthology, Lummox Journal, Poetry Magazine, Poezja Dzisiaj, OccuPoetry,* as well as anthologies by Poets on Site, Southern California Haiku Study Group, the Altadena Library, and others. The Sixth Poet Laureate of Sunland-Tujunga (2010-2012) and the founder of Moonrise Press, Trochimczyk presented her work at over 70 national and international conferences in Poland, France, Germany, Hungary, U.K., Canada, and the U.S. She received fellowships and awards from the American Council of Learned Societies, Social Sciences and Humanities Research Council of Canada, USC, McGill University, MPE Fraternity, the Polish American Historical Association, the City and County of Los Angeles, and Poland's Ministry of Culture and National Heritage. (www.trochimczyk.net).